Sandhya

Sandhya

Or, Songs of Twilight

Dhan Gopal Mukerji

MINT EDITIONS

Sandhya: Or, Songs of Twilight was first published in 1917.

This edition published by Mint Editions 2021.

ISBN 9781513299952 | E-ISBN 9781513223452

Published by Mint Editions®

 MINT
EDITIONS

minteditionbooks.com

Publishing Director: Jennifer Newens
Design & Production: Rachel Lopez Metzger
Project Manager: Micaela Clark
Typesetting: Westchester Publishing Services

Contents

Foreword

Like "Rajani" (perhaps more than), "Sandhya" is a slender rill that has drawn its music from my Bengali which has told upon its English structure. This and many other faults of these poems are due to their unyielding adherence to spontaneity.

"Sandhya" came then, as "Rajani" in its own way through the bed of my Bengali reflecting its sound and sense, and trying to echo back its music that descends on all with the fading twilight.

DHAN GOPAL MUKERJI

N. B.—Since some of these poems were born without, and defy titles, I have refrained from forcing any on them.

Symbolism

Tongueless the bell!
Lute without a song!
It is not night
It is God's dawn,
Silence its unending song.

Over heart's valley,
In the soul's night,
Through pain's window
Behold! His light!
On Life's Height.

No prayer, now,
Though death-waves roll,
Faith's candle lit,
Beside it sits the soul
Reading Eternity's scroll.

Source of Singing

A bruised heart,
A wounded soul,

A broken lute,
That is all!

A sad evening,
And a lone star,

Then song reddens—
Sets life's forest afire!

With purple shadows the mist measures the infinite sea
That spreads her wave-raiment in lavender, violet, gray, and green;
While with thin silver rays a lone star seeks to sound the deeps.

The breeze-wings tire of flight;
The mist-threads weave a rose-fringed dusky drapery
To cover the bare breasts of the dunes from the moon's langour-heavy
    eyes.

The shadows die in purple silence;
Fades the one star from the sky,
As the dark mist puts out the rose-red moon from its deep.

Pale gleams the lighthouse light;
No warring waves break the peace of sleep tonight
Nor a hungry wind shrieks in pain from the lea.

Under her heavy veil of black
A languid sea sluggishly flows
To some far land of forsaken dreams.

"O, Old! O, New!"[1]

Who are you?
Why make me wait
From the hour of dew
Till another sunset?
Why do I look
For your coming?
Listen to the weeping brook
That might bring
To my lonely shore
A word from you.
Ah, nothing! not a leaf's tremor!
O, old! O, longed for new!
Who are you? I ask;
Know not why I seek
From day to dusk
Without waking or sleep,—
No sleep! no waking!
A dreaming, a longing;
Not knowing, yet seeking,
For your coming waiting—
O, spring-born!
O, autumn-clad!
O, soul's new morn!
O, old! O, glad!
So glad, so young!
O, unseen, unknown,
O, fugitive vision!
O, eternal moan
In my heart—

---

1. "O, Old! O, New!" is the cry of a "Poáti," *e. g.*, a mother's cry to her unborn child. "Poáti" has no precise English synonym.

O, tearful Soul of laughter,
Untouched, unhurt,
O, sweet! O, bitter!
My born yet unborn,
Shadow not fallen
O, undawning morn—
O, message unbroken.
Why, how, when?
I wait, wait for you,
O embrace of earth and heaven;
O, Old! O, New!

5

The far away called her—
A pilgrim on the hope-lit bark of youth,
A woman, a child, a soul
On an argosy for the lands of south.

It called her in her dreams;
Her waking into a deeper dream grew;
The flute of the distant
Played ceaselessly the music of the new.

With words of fire it called her,
Beyond the bourne of her days
To a silent sea of joy
Washed by unending twilight-rays.

It called her at dawn
When night shed the star-jewels from her hair;
It called her at sunset
When the moon mutely ascended the heaven's stair.

It called her without ceasing—
Hour after hour but a calling,
Till "Come, come, come!"
At her soul's door kept repeating:

Come, come, come!—in
Her word, her music, her song;
Far away, near, far again
Heedless of nightfall and dawn.

It called, it cried, it prayed,
Till She, the deity, made answer
Through youth, through age, through death
To her own far away's receding star.

DHAN GOPAL MUKERJI

LASSITUDE

Ah! to be able to sing,
To sorrow in melody;
To string with silver
Sorrow's dark harp!

Or, mount every thorn
Crowning life's brow
With lustrous stars—
Those tears of the sky.

Rolling down its face
When night's hand puts
Darkness's crown on its head
As twilight dies.

None of these, for my soul;
Only to weep is given to me,
To nourish my heart's crop
For the scythe of barrenness to reap.

Ah! pale cool lips that burn,
Body that yields, though unyielding,
Oh, moon with the heat of the sun!
Flashing out a million lights
To cleave into nothing the endless firmament of my being.
Take all; my soul's mistress! heart's queen,
The flaming fancies of my dream-tortured night
The intoxicating fruits of my day dream,
The fiery lotus of my senses' delight
That rises from the abyss of my life.
The abysmal heaven of love and living
Now bruised, burnt, torn and thrown
To the winds of thy ravishing rejoicing
Whose inarticulate words of delight and moan
Make the ever-yielding music of my soul.

Forlorn

In the star-blurred hours of the night
When the cloud-dams stay the flow of winds,
Not even the shadow of a meteor moves,
As in the watch-tower of love I sit;
Through the casement of hope look for thy coming
Along the moss-grown path of stones—
Those agonies that time has built on my soul—
By the unfathomable lake of my tears
Shed when even prayers had failed
To bring thy returning.
Come, destroyer of my peace and sleep,
Plunderer of lights of my days!
Enigma on the scroll of my fate
Before the lightnings fired my tower
And thunders crashed in my life's sky.
Only send the echo of thy footfalls—
The ring of thy song,
And a star—reflection of thy smile—
Those million suns in the firmament of my dawn.

After a Bengali Song

In the forest of my being the voice of your lute;
In the depth of my heart the pearl of your tear;
In the temple of my soul chimes the bell of your love.

The fire of dawn, shadow of eve,
Life's sorrow, and death's mute-enchanting peace
Steal away silently, fearfully, at thy flute's music.

O, frail, faint call which I seek to echo!
O, breath of love laden with the aroma of my soul!
Why seek I ever without, O guest at my door?

Moonrise

A soft light mantle of rose wear the brown hills
As they look down on the valley where the rills
Spin their long silver embroideries
For the fringe of spring's greenéd draperies.

The cloud-banks recede with the fading breeze,
The warblers fall into silence in the trees
To listen to many-colored dream-melodies
That the mute stars make on sleep's endless seas.

The last light flickers out of the sky,
Shadows with golden feet o'er the green valley hie;
The silver rills trill like warblers from earth's deeps
As the moon, the sun of another dawn, heavenward leaps.

At Ventura, California

The moon rises and washes the brine with silver;
The dunes like white elephants restfully asleep after the chase;
And the fog comes to bring the moon its veil of shades.
The waves stretch their phosphorescent arms
To embrace the night,
The wind like a wounded gull beats its wings
Over the land, over the sea, into the fog-vested intangibility.

Like a thousand trumpets the breakers
Proclaim the empiry of night,
The rocky caverns send back echoes
Like homage from vassals near and far;
A faint cry seemeth to flash like lightning;
Through the clouds of the roar of waves:
It is not from the rocks, nor from the sea;
Ah! it is the prayer of a mightier ocean—Humanity!

12

The same air that you breathe
Is the air that caresses my sky;
The sunlight that lingers on your hair and lips
Sets fire to the pathway of my life;
And the call of nature's numberless birds
But reflects in world's mirror the music of our heart's singing—
Melody made of sweet agonies,
Exquisite joys poured from pitchers of pain,
As this summer's heat
From the ever-burning heart of heaven.
Not heaven alone;
The earth, the air, flowers, and leaves
Filled with passion that knows no slaking,
Yet tranquil like sleep's dream-billowed sea.
More than dream-billowed sea this love that I bring,
Its boistrous waves seek the firmament of your yielding;
While your heart-beats' arrows seek to slay my heart a'beating,
As I inhale the fragrance of your breath and hair;
And pour the perfume of my soul
On your sun-bathed feet.

Why this return?
Why this sunlight
When all seemed without sun?

Whence this call?
I cannot tell,
Yet its mighty thralls.

Hold me, haunt me
Hour after hour,
With its name of thee.

All seems ended,
The last light lost
In the house of the dead.

Yet with time's tide
Rises thy face,
My heart, my soul, my bride.

Though poureth the rain,
And sorrow clouds my sky,
Yet not mine the pain.

What I hear
I can not tell,
And what I fear,

Will not endure:
But thou returnest,
O serene, O silent, O pure!

By the verge of the woodland,
Where purling brooks loosen their brown tresses,
Where the music of the breeze
Is played on viols of the vines and trees,
Thy soft words I hear
Like songs from enchantment's strings.
Ah, vanishing moments of ecstacy!
Far-fleeing only to be nearer to my soul,
Rest, rest awhile on the hillside of my echoing!
Pour on it the sweet rain of thy words' melody
Till they mingle and drown my tears
Into thy kisses' passion-swept sea.

The Dream of His Soul

The Dream of his Soul, in flesh and blood—
Not to possess, but only to see—
Was given him, for an hour:
Ah, fool, he lingered longer,—
The Dream died like the shadow of a Star!

The Eurasian

Indignity your part today,
Suffering the guerdon of the gods;
No country to claim your own,
Nowhere to lay your head.
The ocean of ignorance separates us;
The snow-storm of commerce blinds the eye;
Yet you must stand true,
Bridge of blood and flesh between the West and East.
In ages to come, when
Man will love his brother,
Irrespective of birth and breed;
In the pantheon of the future, yours the immortal seat.
Son of man, you are brother!
Bearer of the cross of God!
Your destiny the lodestar of our epoch,
Your life our rood-littered road of the Lord.
Arise, awake, halt not
Till the goal is reached;
Raise high the Host of freedom
Blare the trumpet of light.
"Suffer you, for the world to rejoice";
"Die" so they "can live";
Live that you may bring the light
To the meeting place of the West and East.

In the perfumed shrine of love,
Where burns memory's exhaustless incense
From the irridescent thurible of hope,
On the altar and couch of my heart
Rest thy limbs, O, god of my soul.
Drink of the unquenchable draught of caresses;
Tear the flowers of my dreams and fancies;
Scatter the sacred petals of my passion
To the four winds of thy rejoicing.

Thy rejoicing, that one festival of the High Gods,
Where no offering that I bring ever be too dear,
Where no soul burnt in the fire of senses can perish;
Where no suffering fails to be mother and daughter of joy.
Take all, great God among these Gods:
The pearl of my woman-soul buried in deeps of passion,
The coral-wreath from the ocean of my bleeding heart;
And ravish with exquisite merciless touch
The one star in my heaven that has led thee hither—
My life's eternity in this worship of an hour.

The Infirm Beggar Sings

Broken and bruised by the hand of Fate,
    Dark night, my staff,
Leaning on its shadowy strength I walk
    Toward thee, my God.
Thy crescent my e'er-present friend;
    Thy wind, thy voice,
Calls me to go on without end
    To thy star that my soul hath seen.
The hour is black, my road unbuilt;
    My beggar's song
I cannot sing; yet, thou knowest,
    For thy love I long!
I come, O Lord! broken and battered
    To thy world where sorrow is not.

Kiss, my love, kiss
My burning, breaking being;
So when cold death
Will put out the light
In some wilderness
Of far forsaken life
Might each kiss blossom
Into a lotus and a Shephali.[1]
And in the desolate hours
Of loneliness of traveling
In the dusk of despair
One petal of these
Will cheer the vagrant souls
That tread the pathway
Of love's forsaking.
Or, when Death will sow
This Soul of mine
On the lake-shore of sorrow,
Like a weeping willow I will spring,
And with my green tresses
And bending body
Shall shelter secrecy-seeking lovers
That love for an hour,
As our twin hearts today.
Kiss then, with kisses of flame;
Touch me with rosy caresses;
Bury this, my hope, my dream,
And thy all-conquering love of me;
So the kiss-flowers may each be a dream!
May my willow be the vision of Eternal Spring.

---

1. Flowers full of perfume, abounding in Lower Bengal, India.

Color-Harmonies

Violet hills,
Rosy mist,
Limpid pool,
Golden notes from sunset's lute
For shadows
Draped in green
With purple feet
To dance and swim
Through irridescent undulatings.
Dusk descends;
Mauve cloudlets—
Dying butterflies—
Flit and fly and die
In the opalescent ocean of mist
That grows dark and still,
Kisses away the last gold
From the brow of the hills;
Till the coral crescent
With its wand of breeze
Makes silver ripple-music
On the pool's shadow-laden deeps.

SANATAN

(The Absolute)[1]

Our hopes that fail
Are but truths that set
To illumine other spirits on their pathway;
As our joys that come true
Are their far-off dreams,
That through the cadence of our life
Ring out their pent-up tunes.
Whatever dies—needs must live,
Whatever breathes doth die too;
But above death and life
Shines that High Light
Where all find rest,
Yet endlessly move.

---

1. The word *absolute* is the synonym for the Sanskrit word Sanatan, meaning *Eternal and Immutable Truth*.

Coming of the Fog

Killing the light,
Blurring the stars,
Marring the breeze—
Nature's many-stringed harp—

It comes
Silently, sinisterly,
Over the land, over the sea,
Spreading its beggar-raiment of brown.

Without stop, without sound,
Over the valley
Like a great serpent of silence
Coiling around the heart of sound.

A damp insidiousness
Creeps into the night;
A drab numbness sets in
Dripping in lugubrious drops
From the haggard fingers
Of the autumn trees.

It strangles the last sound,
It devours the last light,
Trembles in fear
To see its own visage;

It moves on, on, and around,
Ceaselessly, untiringly,
Till the black night is drowned
In an abyss of brown.

In love's afterglow, full of stars,
Those lilies of the river of night,
Sing no song, dear, speak no word.

The white noontide has ebbed into gold;
Shores-breaking seas cease to roar;
Lo! the moonrise of our soul.

Hardly a kiss, or the shadow of a caress;
No decking the hour with the jasmines of touch;
But a rose-petal shivering in exquisite agony—our love.

The weary sunset has grown wearier;
A vague lassitude encircles us twain,
As separation builds its pathway of tears.

Cease weeping, yet the saffron light lingers;
The stars throb in nebulous lustre,
As our hearts to the music of desire.

What matters if winter be nigh?
We sang summer to sleep,
And autumn on its bed of leaves.

Now comes the hour of parting for us,
As the last light flickers and fades;
Even love's afterglow dying, and is dead.

Alas! thou art gone, as are the hours of day;
The hard gem-burning stars do not set! Oh,
In what dark, in what forest roamest thou?

24

The End

Art thou about me
Amid falling leaves
And autumn's circling winds
When the golden shadows
Grow russet and rosy
And the purple sunset sets fire to the sky?
Art thou the breath
That burns my being
When cold feel my limbs in terror, and awe?
Who art thou? My love?
Stranger in a strange garb!
Far and farther to be nearer to my heart!
Why make spring-flames leap
From passion's autumn leaves?
Why this urge through fatigue
When time falls fast asleep
Under the shadow of its grave—
The winter ice?
Yet, and yet
The circling winds
Repeat passionate speech,
The sunset burns,
As my soul
In desire's golden heat,
Though night be not far
Shadows creep near
With chilling breath and clutching hands
To pluck
To destroy
The flowers of yielding from your heart:
Powerless, fear-stricken;
I tremble, I stagger, I fall

Into oblivion's pit
As time creeps
Into winter's grave
Silent, empty, white.

The Confluence

Tears of Ages come in a stream,
Sighs flow in from Life's hoary height,
Souls of Sorrow bring their gleam
Of a light that is but a moan, not a sight.

The gray waves of the Sea of Death
Congeal under the cold Sun of Suffering,
While Time, playing the flute of Fate,
Charms them, snake-like, and doth bring.

Out of a Cave, beyond Lights and Shades
Present's storm,—made stormier by Future's promises,—
To mingle in the Ocean of Death
Like Sleep, yielding to Dream's caresses.

In the deeps of Dream
O'er the pool of Sleep
A lone star her face
Seeking, with song-kindled eyes
Her Isle of Rest.

Across the dusky hills
The first flush of waking
Unfurls its silver banner
To signal the Isle for her:
She vanishes, as before, into the fading Night.

Thus the Eye of Life
Searches for the home of Peace
Night after night:
And when the sun of Death rises
It flees,—it loves its own night.

To

Leo B. Mihan

Few notes out of the coffer of sound,
An image from the gallery of Nature,
An hour from the infinity of Time,—
Out of these, blessed creature,
Createst thou the world of endless rhyme!

Chopin's Funeral March

The keyboard black and white;
Shadow-Light the Evening's scale;
Half silent the voice of thy singing.
Quiver the notes in pain;
Exquisite, sad, the melody at thy touch;
Like the silver arrow of Desire
Piercing the Soul's golden heart.

The room is lost in dark.
The ivory keys, white fringe
Of a music long since mute;
Yet, in the black night
Tremble and toss notes
Unheard, undreamt,—like sleep
Sleepless, and waking full of smart.

In the golden afterglow you lay,
When the emerald moon
Made thin silver fog-veils
For the bride of night,
Whose saffron-sandled feet
Walked the foam-strewn floor of the sea.
In my arms you listened
To words of love
Poured by the infinite heaven of my heart,
Echoed by the endless symphony of the sky.
Your silent gaze,
Deeper than the song of the sea,
Farther than the moon,
Nearer than your own heart-beat,
Asked mine for speech.
"What can my love say
At this sad sacred hour?"
Hour of parting this!
Love's ever-feared moment,
Longing's much-dreaded end,
Yet no voice sorrows in our being,
No woe dims the moon-face tonight.
Between the sheltering dunes and fading light
On an aërial couch lying,
Adorned in kiss-woven garments of nudity
Our spirits garlanded with myriad embraces,
Borne on passion's flaming wings
Cross this ocean of parting
Unto that far island of Cythera
Where only love reigns
In eternal majesty.

Henrik Ibsen

Lone as the lone north star,
Stern as the rocks that guard the sanctity of his home,
Pure as the white snow of his land,
And beauteous his visions like the fjords
At each turn of the mariner's helm.

The lofty glaciers engage his eyes,
As life's height the sight of his mind;
And his Imagination, expansive as the sea,
Tries to push the boundary-line of the sky, his Soul,
Further and further, where a new North Star
Awaits his exploring eye.

After Hearing "My Old Kentucky Home"

I know not whose the words,
Nor the maker of their music;
    In my sorrow-laden heart
    The aroma of its pathetic art
Like the soothing breath of dream.

Joy borrows its charm from sorrow;
Sorrow feverish with the color of joy;
    An opaque crystal, a stone on life's string
    Made of music that doth ring
As the stars on the lyre of night.

A pain it is, made perfect;
A call made clear by the voice of peace;
    A silver stream of song
    Darkened, yet floweth on and on
Between black banks of memory, into the Soul's white home.

THE COMING OF THE TIDE OF NIGHT

Pale this twilight-face,
Shade-ridden the horizon-light;
The forest, a green-gold vision of grace
In its frame of lavender mist.

No rose-leaf washed in moonlight;
No vine on vermilion walls;
Pale sunlight fading into night,
Dark tunes, the music of the hour.

No death, nor life is ours, here;
But the vast vague sea of black
Sounded by star-mariners
Seeking the Infinite's track.

Dead Love

Pour no blood on ashes, brother,
That is not the way;
Better say nothing,
Blood is no life-giver;
It makes death look so gay.

Dead life, or dead love
Need no blood at all.
No trumpet's call can
Bring back what you lived, and strove:
The ashes know no thrall!

Why cry for a colored glass
That for jewel you took;
The magic—the dream—
All returning to dust and grass,
Not a day love your soul forsook.

At last, you have known it,
That is more than they do.
Be not afraid, O friend,
Alone, alas, alone! you have loved and lived it,
Pour no blood on the ashes, for blood can not turn into dew.

It is the same twilight, dear,
The hour of love and tear
When in raiments of shadows
Fancies, fears, hopes, and sorrows
Tread the path of sunset,
While like barks of jet
Float the clouds from east to west.

I think of thee, my darling,
As in my heart strange chords ring
Out melodies of many memories,
And half-forgotten reveries
Telling of this or that scene,
That is and has been
Trod by thee, Queen of queens.

My dreams of thee are ceaseless,
As my love of thee is endless;
Whether it be sunset or sunrise,
Hour of star-song, or bird-cries
It is of thee that I dream,
In the heart of my soul's stream
That flows to thy feet, my darling.

Dark grows both east and west;
Flower-heads droop into rest,
As I seek to lay my heart and loving
On thy star-white breast, my darling,
And sink into that pool of sleep
That rises from thy singing's deep,
While all are silent, as my desires near thee, my Queen.

What peace thy presence breathes!
What serenity weaves its wreathes!
What myriad wonders touch hands

Across many seas, from many lands,
When a thought of thee
Heralds thy coming to me
Between palpitating desires, and fragrant dreams.

Weariness

Weariness the tune of this evening melody,
Pain the lute to which I sing;
Ah! goddess, why this gray measure
In thy starry harmony?

The white conch[1] of the half-moon
Silent as though all worship's ceased,
No incense-perfume from the forest censer
The breeze brings; all still, like torrid noon.

I row in a black bark on a copper-colored sea,
The sun fades like a golden bubble in its deep;
Weariness the chart that I hold in my hand,
Weariness the tune of this evening melody.

---

1. In a Hindu temple conch shells are blown during or at the close of a worship.

36

A call, not a song;
A command, not a prayer;
No mellowing moonlight, but dawn,
Frail, fanciful, and fair
In the east of my dream and desire.
At the portal of unending desire,
Draped in diaphanous dreams,
With a whispered word of fire
That quivers and gleams
Through the clouds of my longing.
Longings poignant with pains and tears
Enfold, and fill my soul
That aches with hopes and fears
As thy chariot wheels' roll
Sets fire with torches of gold
To my words, my silences, my singing,
And to this black pyre of my life
To take my being on the wings of thy embracing
To sail away, far away from man's hate and strife
Where only love reigns on its throne of unending light.

Remorse

Gently descending dark—
Curtain of silence
From heaven to earth;

The drama of day over,
Empty the seats of life,
Dead the twilight fire.

Curtains of black
Woven from threads of purple
By the hands of a star,

That lone soul weeping
Over the dead hours
Laid by mute time in the eternal's grave.

In the night of my soul
Not even a ray,
Nor a mourner present;

But a deep dark hollow
Where no fate weeps
Even fear is afraid to tread:

Fear-forsaken, hollow within hollow,
Even silence flees from me—
O, the pity of it!

DHAN GOPAL MUKERJI

Poet

To distil a few golden drops of song
Through the gloom of this hour;
To filter true emotions
Through passion's burning fire
When the sun bubble-like fades in the west;
As our being craves for night's rest
That pool of silver in life's forest of distress.

To light some pale candles
In the cavern of a lonely isle
And draw the wine of day
From the must of midnight,
Or plant a star-seed in the gray-ploughed eve—
So out of the abyss of the blackness of night
Dawn's million-colored fountain might spring.

Wanderer

The silvery beach, a riband around the flowing hair of the sea,
Where gleam the foam-flowers garlanded in multitudinous nebulous
    rings:
Here, on the frontier of many worlds and the billow-rocked cradle of
    eternal sleep,
No sound, no music, no silence that a wounded soul can heal.

A longing more tempestuous than the craven breeze-possesséd deep,
And tears that outweigh the salt of the woeful brine,
Yet no sleep dream-robbed, or dream-laden, nor even death's pallid
    peace;
But a ceaseless crying over my heart's forsaken valleys
Where love like a wraith haunts the empty tombs of memory.

At Dawn

With the breath of dawn
Cooling thy feverish brow,
And the fading of the last footfall of the stars
No kiss can I bring to thy bedside,
Nor caresses of cooling fire, my sweet.
Yet through this dreamful silence
That writes on the rim of the golden light
The story of our love
With most eloquent poignancy,
More love we pour into each other
Than the tryst of an eternal night.

From her many-colored bow Nature
Has hurled her silver arrows of rain
And slain the hosts of Dark.

Jeweled with a single star, the Moon
Walks the garden of Night;
Higher and higher
Through the star-enflowered pathways of sapphire
She draws her train of silver.

DHAN GOPAL MUKERJI

42

If words fail, song will come;
If thought fades, souls will not be dumb;
If sound ceases, Silence our song;
If Life fails,—Death join our hands.

Rainy Night

Like tears shed over a dream,
Like sighs that stream
In an unseen nameless way
Into the heart of our lay.

It seemed hour on hours,
Years like fading flowers
Scattered their petals and bloom
In a half-lit forest of gloom.

The softness of its sounds,
Like the coursing of a million hounds
Of dream over the glade of sleep
Where tortured silences creep.

Exquisite, pain-laden, peaceful,
This night most beautiful,
What love forsaken by loving
Sets his heart a'singing?

No torment in it, but tenderness;
A liquid star-music of sadness
Pours into my soul half asleep;
While the willows at my window weep.

Ghosts

Flames flickered in the fireplace,
As memories on the hearth of life;
Two shadows we, watching, brooding,
To catch our reflection
In a non-existent stream.

The ghost-witness of it all,
The clock brings its proofs;
Moments melt into moments,
Like notes of sad music,
Like a white cerement.

Cold memories shroud our life;
Speech flees before this;
Faces turn away from each other;
The fire throws light on them;
There, too, flames burn and flicker.

RAIN

What world-agony distils its poignancy this day?
What pain-laden heart pours out its exhaustless lay
Of tormenting woe and tortured silences?

From the far reaches of the marshland
Along and beyond the crescent-bed of the sea-sand
What tempest on the wave's-strings makes its cadences?

The distant hills dimmed like dull and forgotten dreams
Raise their shadowy heads where pour in streams
The tears of the heart-hollowed mourners of the skies;

While into the turgid heart of the fens at their feet
Turbidly fall and dance sheet upon sheet
To the measureless measure of the wind's empty sighs.

No light but a dismal gray, that neither throbs nor quivers
On the torn banks of the heavens' cloud-rivers,
But stonily stands still, like death that dies never.

Not-dead, but a weeping world bathing its corpses—
Its memories, its lost hopes, in regret's hearses
To be buried in flowerless graves, without incense or prayer.

It writhes in agony, rolls out in undulating rills,
This rain-melody from the sea-waves to the farthest hills,
Thence to the dreary distance lost to hearing or sight.

It is all dark and dank, a mourning of earth and heaven,
Sorrow-laden, life-weary, long-lost, death-craven,
A day lost to time, a light more baleful than night.

No dead these, but a living death seeking peace
From the furies—their own thoughts—sorrow—surcease,
Kissing the lashing wind thinking it to be the breeze.

Pour, pour, pour, O relentless, exhaustless pain!
To the measure of thine own agony, thy woe's refrain,
These desolate streams of thy music, thy pangs of a million seas.

Evening Worship

The amber west melts into saffron,
The east, a misty vision of rose:
Like the sun, our souls seek repose.
The mountains, empurpled priests,
The river, the chant from their lips,
Sunlit the pine-candles' crimson tips.

At this hour of worship
Shadows spread their wings;
Silently the breeze-bell rings.
The stars put a silver riband round night's tresses,
The light fades like a receding song
As fall soundless sounds from Nature's
moon-gong.

DHAN GOPAL MUKERJI

The rosy mist stilly polishes the round mirror,
       The moon;
       Golden her face

Reflecting the cool sweet glory of a
       Baby sun
       When dangling

His short golden arms in the cradle of the sky
       After night
       Gave him birth,

And herself died as day dies to see the moon,
       This golden
       Rose-washed stone

That the unseen hand puts on the crown of night
       Beside it puts
       Bits of white—

The star-jewels like million fancies, worshipping
       The goddess
       Of dream.

The sun's golden spear,
The violet cloud writhing in pain;
Golden the tint of the sky,
The tall trees wave their green-gold hair.

Music of this hour!
The zephyr's perfume-laden argosy
Drifts with the song of lutes
Down the sunset-stream that falls from heaven's bower.

Another flow of light,
Tinkling like the intangible bells of paradise,
Flows out of my heart
Into the mysterious love-perfumed ocean of night.

TRUCE

A field of battle—this sky,
The sun, the hero bleeding to death;
The shadows and lights hurl their
Hosts of clouds ceaselessly:
No peace?
Warfare all?
Nay, lo! she cometh—
The Spirit of Truce,
The Evening Star!

A PARALLEL

Time has passed, since
Shadows trembled to watch
Twilight sweep the earth
For the phantoms to trip and mince.

A dark breeze the forest-heart stirs;
Yet merry the face of the sky—
Twinkling in joy
Its innumerable eyes, the stars.

Hushed the music within;
Pleasure's silver laugh, dead;
Thought lost in reverie—
Reverie receding into nothing.

The taper of dreams flickers
Out, leaving the soul in dusk
By the altar of love,
Flower-laden as the night with stars.

"Nothing endures," you said;
"None can die," quoth love;
"In the firmament of loving
 No stars set, no meteors fall."

Yet, nothing endures, nothing,
 Naught but dust;
 Naught but regret and vain desire
 The twin monuments of life,

Reared by time, by wrecking
All that we seek and find.
Its relentless waves of years
Break even the impregnable wall of memory
That thought builds
On the embankment of hope.

Pass all away, even we who loved,
Dreamt as none dreamt before—
Borne by the tide of life—
But, lo! from our defeated destiny
Rise our seeds reared by time
Consecrated to love and living!

Disappointment

They think thee bitter:
Thou art not made o' laughter
Nor love's smile
Can thy vision beguile:
Like a black-fiery comet
Suddenly, sinisterly, thou comest;
Making thy fateful journey,
Littering the floor of destiny
With wreckages of life,
Of love, of heart—
Of all visitors thou art the surest;
Halting nowhere long, endlessly passest,
Dragging behind thee thy train of fire
That burneth all, heedless of curse or prayer.

Buddha

On thy Lotus-seat of Night,—
Meditation closing thy eyes,—
The Star Hosts thy awe-struck devotees:
The Moon, thy halo unchanging.
White-robed time telling his beads
Of aeons on the thread of Eternity
By the ocean of space
Slumbering in peace at thy feet;
While Destiny stringing the lyre of death
Sings Nirvana's hymn.

Ask me not to stand at thy friendship's gate—
I, who loved thee, now must like a cold spectre from a far forgotten
    land of snow
Watch thee fall asleep on the couch of freezing friendship?
In these arms thou sought and joyed on many delights
Excavated the ruins of passion to build them anew,
Or sailed on thy wings—these arms—over love's enchanted sea.
                Friendship!
Barrier not this, but a coward's refuge—
A shadow, not the rainbow-light of loving and life.
O come, my pilot, conduct the bark of our twin souls
From cold friendship's haven
Over love's boistrous desire-foam-fringéd ocean
Till in the sheer joy and fatigue of flying
We fail, fall and fade
Into the heart of Passion's another fire-born day.

Golden vines they,
These thin lines of light,
Climbing the sky-wall
After the sun sank into sleep.

Like rills, thread-like,
Seen from a jutting rock
Where air is dizzy
And fancy infinite, free.

What fiery wine
Tingles in these vines
Weaving golden arabesques
On the pale evening sky?

Ah, the heavens this hour
Have drunk of sunset's ruby Wine
For those golden cobwebs to weave
Their magic of twilight dreams.

At Sundown

Two shadows fell, tremulous and frail,
From the upland over the lake-surface pale,
While the shivering reeds shook at sunset,
As the swans sailed into a sea of jet.

The rippling waters, and the breeze,
And the shadows that fall from the trees,
Mingled and melted with the twain,
A song of whitewashed away by its black refrain.

Only words remained, palpitating and few,
Falling through the gloom and night's dew
Like jewelled fancies rising out of a dream
That live for a moment and die ere they gleam.

Tears well out from my heart,
As clouds overcast my soul,
And blur my vision of thee.

Melancholy this dawn,
When thy smile and words,
And thy sky-shaming eyes
Are not beside me to rouse me from sleep.

Though cry I without end,
Yet a thought of thee heals many wounds,
Why? thou ask me; how can I tell?

All thou wish to take is thine;
Not even the dust of thy feet I seek,
Only leave me the star of thy memory
To bathe in the rain of my weeping.

At last thou comest;
Thy footsteps I hear across the ages,
Over wandering fancies,
Through shadows of dreams
Is thy coming, Queen of queens.

This shimmering summer of life
That thou bringest with thee
As a gift to my silent waiting
Is but what I prayed to bring
To the altar of thy coming.

I spread the seat of my soul,
For thee to rest thy tired limbs;
And wave the fan of my heart
To cool thy lotus-shaming face,
Lady of light, queen of grace.

Come to my bower of worship,
Where burns the incense of devotion,
Lay thy rose-robed body
In the shrine of my longing,
Where love's rainbow-songs are ringing.

59

The lingering light of the sun
Takes from the chalice of the valley
Its mist-perfume to wash the
Moon-face with rose.
In the pool at my feet the goldfishes drag their trains of brown
Which cleave it into parts that ceaselessly mingle anew.
The moon, silver bright
Through thousand streams sends her light
Into the valley aswoon, listening to the harmony of night.

I have drunk your tears with insatiate lips;
I have broken like a toy the heart of your life;
What have I given? your last query!
The cup of my heart filled I with love;
The chalice of soul with the substance of my God,
For thee to drink my life's first love.
Thou drankest as one that comes from a desert,
Thou spiltest the nectar heedless, like mad;
Yet I cursed not, nor shed tears;
But loved thee, longed to live for thy love.
Alas! thy tears grew salt, thy love thy self's greedy grasp,—
O, it is the end; let us part!
The morning of indifference wings the gray sky;
The bird-song of the other dawns the raven's shriek now,—
Shed no more tears, I tire of my drink;
Break not thy heart; thy soul? Let it be still!
Beyond the gray-cloud is the land of sunrise:
Let us part, dear, let us be wise.

Sound Butterflies

(In a Fountain)

Like interpenetrating bells of silver,
The water-drops ring and melt
Into new drops, like new notes
From an untiring lyre,
That in colored succession
Paint our heart-beats
From the gold of sunrise into sunset fire;
Yet, not like that, this brush of water-drops
Limns on the silver rim of Joy
The dark Butterflies of Desire.

Even in sadness thou art beside me,
In gladness, none so happy as thee;
    I love thee;
May my love kiss the feet of thy love of me.

My dreams are thine, day or night,
My sleep sings in silence to the night
    Of thy delight;
May thy heart's gifts like stars my heart's heaven bedight!

Though a sigh rises in my soul this hour;
Closes its petals in the west the golden day-flower;
    In my bower
Let thy love pour its rainbow shower.

By the sea of sleep walks white-robed Night;
The breeze but the faint rustle of her drapery
That calls the mist-made bark of dream
From the cavern of the Unknown to sail to us,
Laden with endless star-like fancies.
And She! the magician, walks on and on
Over the sapphire embankment of the sky
Like a moving magnet drawing behind her a million dream-argosies.

64

Farewell

(After a Hindustani Song)

Farewell, fairest of loves!
Life's most fanciful of gifts,
Joy and treasure, love and wonder,
Waking's elusive reality,
Dream's ever-yielding divinity.
Even thou must pass
Beyond time's starless bar:
Thy eyes, their lambent flames
Shall no more illumine my night;
Nor thy brow, home of many moods,
Tranquil yet tormented as a sea,
Shall ever wear the coronal of my kiss.
Ah, kisses! blisses of fire,
Passion's long lingering melody
Played by thy lips on mine.
Even they must die—
Intangible realities of rapture,
Ever present wonders of desire—
Now like autumn leaves
Fly with the west-wind of fear.
No, not fear that takes thee from me,
Nor love's slayer, satiety;
Yet art gone; thou art going.
Oh, not to crush thy heart on mine:
Thy breasts made but for my hands,
No more to quiver in rapture therein!
Who wills this cruel decree?
The warmth of thy body,
The staggering storm of thy yielding,
The intoxicating perfume of thy mouth:
These, and many other endless

78   DHAN GOPAL MUKERJI

Viols and lutes of passion, love, life,
Delights of a thousand heavens,
Who robs them of me?
Fate! that fool in the court of love,
Who hath no wit for laughter,
Steals it all from me
In the mid-hour of life;
And as it befits his mind,
Scatters it all over the turbid
Stream of fear and lies.

Satiety

All thy gifts must die,
All thy thoughts must fail;
Such were the decree writ by time
With shadows on the scroll of fate.
Even thy memory recedes into forgetting,
Thy lustrous words star-like set,
Ah, sweet! autumn's breath withers all,
Even the west-wind fears to tread.
All yield to the power of relentless time
That no love nor passion can stay,
Blown like dried leaves we now
On the granite pavement of fate.
No more thy lip-touch on my brow,
Nor thy hands pleading caresses,
Thy gifts fall and fade into nothing,
Thy vision grows dim in life's sunset-west.

Drowsy the noonday air,
Under the trees the still shadow
Like a fugitive fragment of night
Seeks shelter from the sun.

The bird has ceased singing,
The beggar unable to bear
The wealth of the sun
Spreads his torn garment,

To find peace in
The benign shadow of sleep.
Ah, lone soul like him,
I spread this rag of my song.

Under the tree of life
Over which blazes the sun of fate.
The calm of its shadow
Protects me, but where my peace?

CHATTERTON

For summers seventeen
This flower of spring
Scattered fragrance
That dwelt in its petals seventeen.
Seventeen song-hours,
A heart never weary;
A soul with honey of all flowers
A song as enchanting as stars.

A boy never grown old,
A lute never tiring to sing,
A mind ne'er chilled
Though Hunger's hand lay cold.

Steely-cold on his breast,
Yet the boy sang;
Loved as alone a poet can
Endlessly, without rest.
Just seventeen!
Ne'er old, though time passes;
A golden lyre-string
Has not yet ceased ringing:

Rings through the heart of time
O'er the summit of death
To the music of the Nine
Into the heart of Eternal Rhyme.

68

A summer song it was,
Counting of many unseen stars
In an intangible sky
Making new milky ways—
Silver-shadow-paths that lead
From sapphire abysses
Into deeper abysses still.
The deeps of our souls
Lit by passion's burning flowers
Tremulous, timorous flames of silver,
That with thousand hands
Our hearts sought to pluck and scatter,
Or make barbéd garlands
For love's nuptial hour.
Nuptial hour, briefer than a moment,
Longer than Heaven's Eternal summer,
When each flower burns to soothe,
And each soothing petal burns anew;
Till myriad streams of fire
Strewn with countless flaming stars
Bear us to the far sea of Time
Where no summer dies,
Nor endure the stinging moments of love's winter.

"Who Knows"

Time's torment,
Life's woes,
And sorrow's wan gaze
Are but shades
In a picture of light
Where nothing abides,
All things fade.
In fading there is beauty,
By shedding tears
We bathe our hearts—
Those crushed flowers full of smart—
For a deity not far from our souls.
Yet, no solace in prayer,
Pain has no largess;
Dark has stars,
But no barren earth its flowers.
All are dismal and fallow;
Yet, from the mountain's stony heart
Spring multitudinous rivers
Sparkling at dawn, and
Deepening night's gloom with mysterious murmurs;
And who knows?
These streams that pass
By the balcony of our past,
Through present's wilderness,
Into desolate future
May reach the land of the farthest star.
Who knows? Ah! who knows?
May these song-rills
From my heart's little hill
Empty their singing waters
Into a sea of song-making
Where nothing endures

DHAN GOPAL MUKERJI

But the sound and echo of singing.
Where sound, and echo are one,
A moonset vale of sunset land,
Where light is wedded to shade
Without death, full of dying, yet not dead.

The First Vision

The impenetrable dark—
Darkness of cloud and night
Coming on black silent wings
Surround me in their folds,
As it sits by my side on the shore of time.

No fear, no sorrow, no hope,
Not even the footfall of a star;
Dim, deep sable tones
Rise from the organ of nothing
With its flats and sharps of clouds and night.

Ripples of moments
Waves of hours and years
Break on the shore of space
To speak vague, soundless words
To my soul, alone, shade among shades.

Not even the unheard whisper
Of the shadow of a breeze,
But silence ponderous, peaceful,
Afraid of its own self
A mute hound at my feet.

Who art thou?
Whom do I know in this emptiness?
Who has lived with me?
And called me from the deeps of time?

Recedes the bank of space;
Fades away even the unfilled time,
No light, no sound, not even a dream;

Yet who speaks through silence?
Who plays this music of night?

Like an intangible river it flows
With waves of shadow-sound
Between banks of mountainous silence—
O, who! who are you?
Light in a world of shadows,
Rainbow among sunless clouds,
Bark of song on this sea of silence,
O ferryman of the soul!
O Word on Infinite's scroll.

SHANTI[1]

Sleep shadows, sleep light;
Sleep tune, sleep speech;
Sleep night, sleep day;
Sleep children in the cradle of rest.

Dream stars, dream moon;
Dream sea; dream O, sun;
Dream rainbow, dream storm;
Dream rain, O, milk from Heaven's breast.

Rest ye feet, rest ye hands;
Rest bleeding hours of even;
Rest O, heart torn and burnt,
Rest my fancies, day is done.

Sleep night, sleep with star-eyes closed;
Sleep sorrow in death's silent repose;
Sleep O, Soul, be it twilight or morn;
Sleep thou too, O, sleep, heedless of moon and sun.

---

1. Shanti is the Sanskrit for "Peace."

A Note About the Author

Dhan Gopal Mukerji (1890–1936) was an Indian American writer. Born near Calcutta, Mukerji was the son of a former lawyer who devoted himself to music and prayer. A member of the Brahmin caste, Mukerji spent a year living an ascetic lifestyle before enrolling at the University of Calcutta, where he joined a group of Bengali revolutionaries with his older brother Jadugopal. In 1910, Mukerji was sent to Japan to study industrial engineering, which he soon abandoned to emigrate to the United States. Settling in San Francisco, he joined the local bohemian community of anarchists and artists while studying at the University of California at Berkeley and later Stanford. In his time in California, he published two books of poems—*Sandhya: Or, Songs of Twilight* (1917) and *Rajani, or Songs of the Night* (1922)—and a musical play, *Laila Majnu* (1922). Mukerji graduated in 1914 with a degree in English, married artist Ethel Ray Dugan in 1918, and moved to New York City in the early 1920s. There, he embarked on a career as a popular children's book author, finding success with *Kari the Elephant* (1922) and *Gay Neck, The Story of a Pigeon* (1927), winning the 1928 Newbery Medal from the American Library Association for the latter. Recognized as the first popular writer of Indian origin in the United States, Mukerji struggled with marginalization and racism and regretted his exile from India late in life. Unable to return because of his youthful commitment to revolutionary politics, he supported the Indian independence movement with money and advocacy from abroad. Ultimately, he ended his life alone in his apartment in New York City.

A Note from the Publisher

Spanning many genres, from non-fiction essays to literature classics to children's books and lyric poetry, Mint Edition books showcase the master works of our time in a modern new package. The text is freshly typeset, is clean and easy to read, and features a new note about the author in each volume. Many books also include exclusive new introductory material. Every book boasts a striking new cover, which makes it as appropriate for collecting as it is for gift giving. Mint Edition books are only printed when a reader orders them, so natural resources are not wasted. We're proud that our books are never manufactured in excess and exist only in the exact quantity they need to be read and enjoyed.

bookfinity™

Discover more of your favorite classics with Bookfinity™.

- Track your reading with custom book lists.
- Get great book recommendations for your personalized Reader Type.
- Add reviews for your favorite books.
- AND MUCH MORE!

Visit **bookfinity.com** and take the fun Reader Type quiz to get started.

Enjoy our classic and modern companion pairings!

Classic & Modern